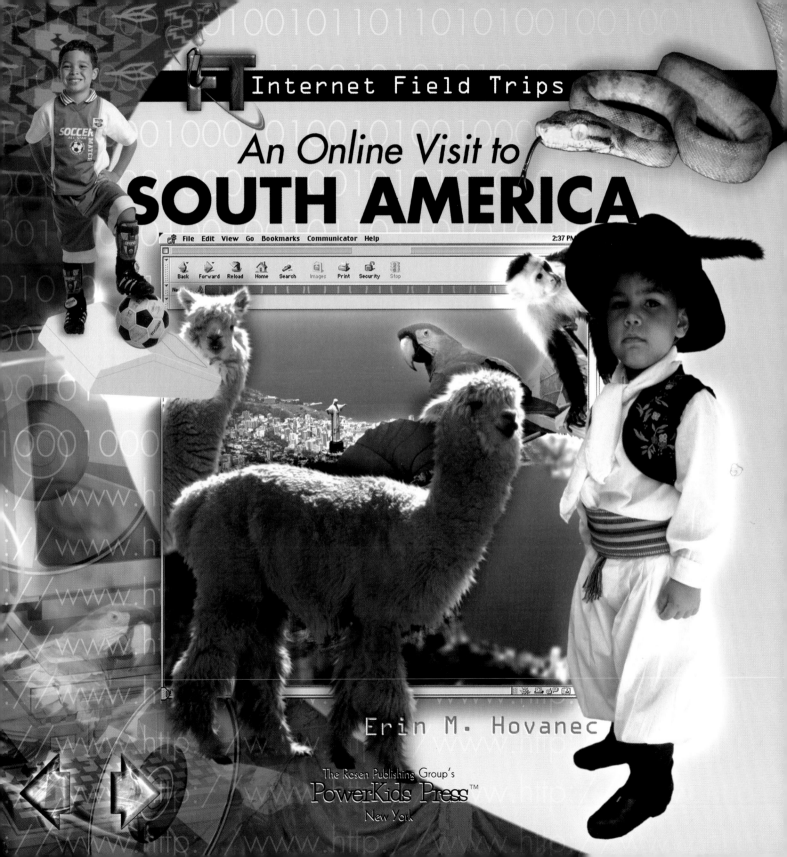

Internet Field Trips

An Online Visit to
SOUTH AMERICA

File Edit View Go Bookmarks Communicator Help   2:37 PM

Back Forward Reload Home Search Images Print Security Stop

Erin M. Hovanec

The Rosen Publishing Group's
PowerKids Press™
New York

In memory of my grandmother, Joan Conway

Published in 2001 by The Rosen Publishing Group, Inc.
29 East 21st Street, New York, NY 10010

First Edition

Book Design: Maria Melendez

Photo Credits: Cover, title page, Child in Cowboy Costume © Barnabas Bosshart/CORBIS; title page, Alpacas Graze in Valley © Galen Rowell/CORBIS; title page, Amazon Tree Boa © David A. Northcott/CORBIS; title page, Woven Folk Art Textiles © Owen Franken/CORBIS; title page, Scarlet Macaw in a Papaya Tree © Steve Kaufman/CORBIS; title page, White-faced Capuchin monkey © A. LittleJohn/H. Armstrong Roberts; title page, Rio Brazil © International Stock; p. 11 (Open air art market) © K. Scholz/H. Armstrong Roberts; p. 20 (Carnival in Rio Brazil) © IPP/H. Armstrong Roberts; p. 15 (Keel-Billed Toucan) © T. Ulrich/H. Armstrong Roberts; p. 19 (Coffee plantation) © Paulo Fridman/International Stock; p. 16 (Youth in Brazil) © Paulo Fridman/International Stock; p. 12 (Amazon Brazil) © Paulo Fridman/International Stock; p. 7 (Machu Picchu, Peru) © Ric Ergenbright/CORBIS; p. 8 (Andes, Patagonia) © Hubert Stadler/CORBIS.

Hovanec, Erin M.
   An online visit to South America / Erin M. Hovanec.—1st ed.
     p. cm. — (Internet field trips)
   Includes index.
   Summary: An online trip to various Internet web sites reveals a variety of facts about the continent of South America.
   ISBN 0-8239-5655-5 (alk. paper)
   1. South America—Computer network resources—Juvenile literature. 2. Web sites—Directories—Juvenile literature. 3. World Wide Web (Information retrieval system)—Juvenile literature. [1. South America.] I. Title.

F2208.5 .H68 2001
025.06'98—dc21   00-028590

Manufactured in the United States of America

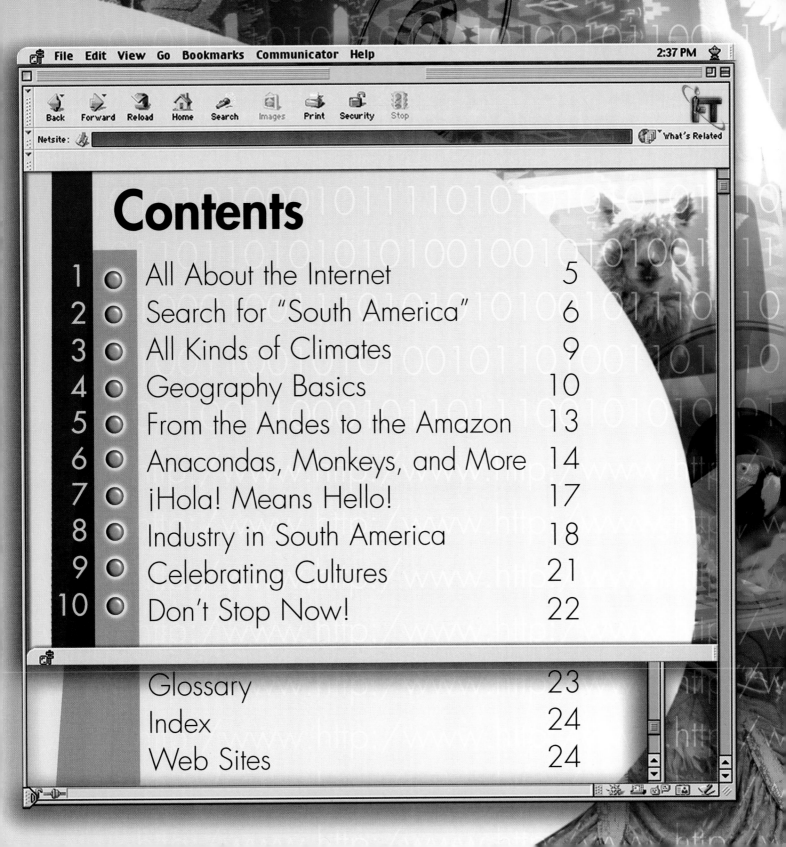

Back   Forward   Reload   Home   Search   Images   Print   Security   Stop

Netsite: What's Related

Contents

Getting Started

If you have a computer at home, you can get on and search the Internet. You can also use a computer at your school or public library. To start surfing the Net, here's what you'll need:

A personal computer
A computer with a monitor or screen, a mouse, and a keyboard.

A modem
A modem to connect your computer to the telephone line, and then to other computers.

A telephone connection
This will enable your modem to "talk" to other computers through a telephone line.

Internet software
These programs tell your computer how to use the Internet.

An Internet Service Provider
ISP companies allow you to get on the Internet.

All About the Internet

Take a hike up the Andes mountains. Sail the Amazon River. Celebrate Carnival in Brazil. You can do all these things, and more, by clicking onto the Internet! People often call the Internet the "World Wide Web," the "Net," or just the "Web." The Internet is a huge connection of computers around the world. You can search the Web to find just about anything you've ever wanted to know. A computer program called a search engine sorts through millions of pieces of information to find what you want. Enter the words "South America" and a list of colored words called hyperlinks will appear. These hyperlinks will connect you to Web sites about South America.

5

Search for "South America"

South America is one of seven **continents** on Earth. Although South America is huge, almost seven million square miles (18 million square km) in size, it is only the fourth largest continent. It is part of a region of Earth called Latin America. The Caribbean Sea lies northwest of South America. The Atlantic Ocean lies along its east coast. The Pacific Ocean lies along its west coast. The continents of North and South America are connected by a narrow land bridge called the Isthmus of Panama. Drake's Passage, a body of water at the southern tip of South America, separates it from the continent of Antarctica.

6

The globe shows the continent of South America. This photo shows the ruins of Machu Picchu, an ancient city in Peru. ▶

To learn more about the continent of South America:
http://www.nationalgeographic.com/xpeditions/main.html
http://www.eplay.com/1999-06-19/mapit-zapit

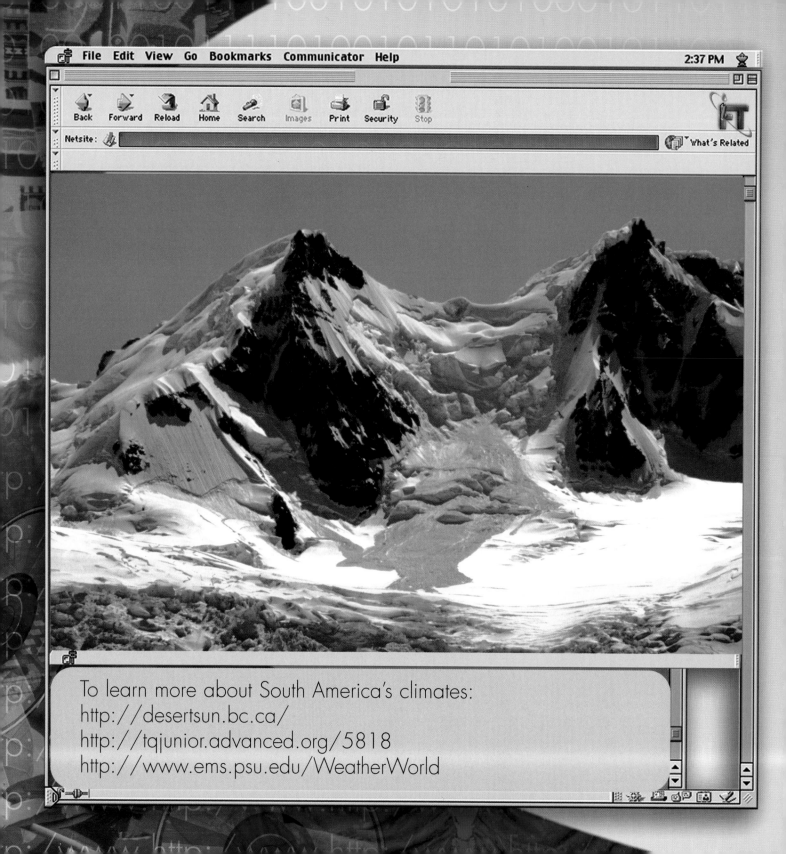

File   Edit   View   Go   Bookmarks   Communicator   Help   2:37 PM

Back   Forward   Reload   Home   Search   Images   Print   Security   Stop

Netsite: What's Related

To learn more about South America's climates:
http://desertsun.bc.ca/
http://tqjunior.advanced.org/5818
http://www.ems.psu.edu/WeatherWorld

All Kinds of Climates

South America has almost every kind of **climate**, from wet, tropical **rain forests** to hot, dry deserts. The **equator** runs through the continent. Most of the countries are in the **tropics** and are warm year-round. The hottest temperature recorded on the continent was in Rivadavia, a town in Argentina, where the temperature reached 120 degrees Fahrenheit (49 degrees C) on December 11, 1905. The part of the Atacama Desert in Calama, Chile, is one of the driest places on Earth. The high, snow-topped peaks of the Andes mountains have cold weather year-round while the Amazon rain forest is usually hot and steamy.

Peaks in the Andes are covered with snow year-round. The Andes mountain range is the longest mountain chain in the world.

Geography Basics

More than 500 million people live in South America. That may seem like a lot, but it's actually less than nine percent of the world's **population**. Three-fourths of South America's population live in cities. São Paulo, the capital of Brazil, is the continent's largest city. More than 10 million people live in São Paulo, making it the third largest city on Earth. South America has 13 separate countries. Brazil is the largest, at 3.3 million square miles (8.5 million square km). Suriname is one of the smallest, at 63,000 square miles (163,200 square km). Argentina, Chile, Colombia, Peru, and Venezuela are among the largest countries in South America.

10

This open-air art show, called "La Boca," is in the South American city of Buenos Aires, Argentina. ▶

To learn more about South America's geography:
http://www.eduweb.com/amazon.html
http://www.3datlas.com/main_gl.html

To learn more about the Andes and the Amazon:
http://www.EnchantedLearning.com/subjects/rainforest
http://www.eplay.com/1998-12-2/etravel/places/place3.adp

From the Andes
TO THE AMAZON

South America has two of the most exciting regions on Earth. The Andes mountain range stretches for 5,500 miles (8,851 km). At the southern tip of the Andes, Aconcagua Mountain in Argentina rises to 22,831 feet (6,959 m), making it the tallest mountain in the Western **Hemisphere**. The Amazon region is just as amazing as the Andes, but it's much hotter! The Amazon rain forest grows in the Amazon River Basin, which covers two-fifths of South America. This rain forest has a very hot, wet climate, making it a perfect home for many plants and animals. Rain forests contain more types of plants than anywhere else on Earth.

◄ *The Amazon rain forest has more than 2,500 different kinds of trees and many rare flowers.*

13

Anacondas, Monkeys,
AND MORE

Have you ever seen a manatee? How about a tapir? Both of these unusual animals live in South America. Many of the continent's most interesting animals live in the Amazon rain forest. These include armadillos, giant anteaters, and many kinds of monkeys. One of the world's largest snakes, the anaconda, lives there, too. It can grow up to 30 feet (9 m) long. Beautiful birds, such as flamingos, parrots, and toucans live in South America. You can find electric eels, giant otters, and piranha, which are flesh-eating fish, swimming in its waters. Lots of llamas live there, too. Llamas are trained to carry goods on their backs.

14

This toucan is one of many beautiful birds found in the Amazon rain forest. ▶

To learn more about South America's animals:
http://mbgnet.mobot.org/sets/rforest/animals/index.htm
http://www.jackiewild.com
http://www.animnalsoftherainforest.com

File   Edit   View   Go   Bookmarks   Communicator   Help   2:37 PM

Back   Forward   Reload   Home   Search   Images   Print   Security   Stop

Netsite: What's Related

To learn about South American people and children:
http://www.LittleExplorerers.com/Spanish
http://www.geographia.com/indx05.htm
http://www.ccph.com/cota

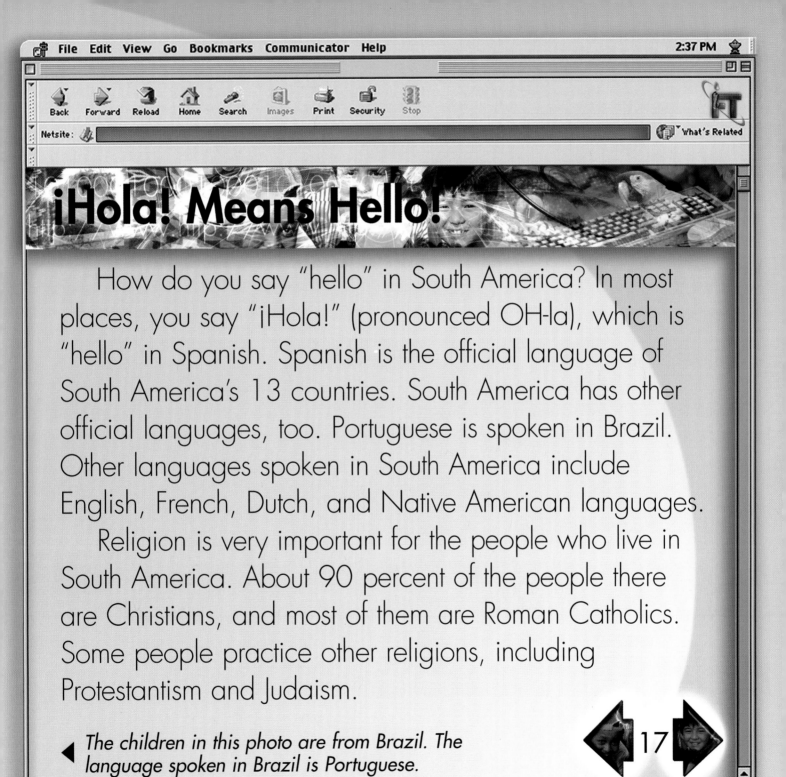

¡Hola! Means Hello!

How do you say "hello" in South America? In most places, you say "¡Hola!" (pronounced OH-la), which is "hello" in Spanish. Spanish is the official language of South America's 13 countries. South America has other official languages, too. Portuguese is spoken in Brazil. Other languages spoken in South America include English, French, Dutch, and Native American languages.

Religion is very important for the people who live in South America. About 90 percent of the people there are Christians, and most of them are Roman Catholics. Some people practice other religions, including Protestantism and Judaism.

The children in this photo are from Brazil. The language spoken in Brazil is Portuguese.

17

South American countries participate in many different **industries**. Brazil is a very rich country that manufactures goods to sell in South America and the rest of the world. Cars, computers, and televisions are produced there. Other countries, such as Argentina and Chile, manufacture goods, too. Many trees from the Amazon River Basin are used to make furniture, nuts, oils, and rubber. **Agriculture** is also important. South America's farmers produce bananas, coffee, cocoa, soybeans, and sugar. Mining is also a major industry in South America. The continent has huge deposits of copper, gold, iron, petroleum, and other valuable **minerals**.

South America has some of the largest farms in the world. These people are working on a coffee plantation. ▶

To learn about South American industries:
http://www.odci.gov/cia/publications/factbook
http://tqjunior.advanced.org/3901
http://www.sdnhm.org/kids/minerals/cover.html

To learn more about the art of South America:
http://library.thinkquest.org/50055/brazil.htm

Celebrating Cultures

Where can you find the biggest party on Earth? You can find it in Brazil. The city of Rio de Janeiro, hosts an enormous celebration called Carnival every February. It is a traditional Christian celebration. People dress in colorful costumes and parade through the streets. Argentina is famous for its dance, the tango. That country's artists also produce beautiful paintings and sculptures. Chile is famous for its literature and poetry, as well as for its folk music and rodeos. South American Indians are admired for their skillful work with clay, cloth, feathers, and stone. The continent's stone churches and cathedrals are some of the most wonderful in the world.

During Carnival, people dress in colorful costumes and parade through the streets, singing and making music.

21

Don't Stop Now!

In South America, you can find some of the most exciting natural wonders on Earth. Would you want to take a trip through a hidden gold mine? Would you rather discover the secrets of ancient South American peoples? You can do all this and more on the Internet.

If you want to know more about this fascinating part of the world, start at Britannica.com at http://www.britannica.com. There you'll find information on everything from anacondas to anteaters, from mining to mountains, from Spanish-speaking people to the country of Suriname. There's always more to learn about South America. This continent is always changing.

22

G L O S S A R Y

agriculture (A-grih-kul-cher) Farming and raising animals.

climate (KLY-mit) The kind of weather a certain area has.

continents (KON-tin-ents) The seven great masses of land on Earth.

equator (ih-KWAY-tur) An imaginary line around Earth that separates it into two parts, North and South. The area around the equator is always hot.

hemisphere (HEH-muh-sfeer) A half of Earth's surface.

industries (IN-des-trees) Businesses that make a product or provide a service.

minerals (MIN-er-uhls) Natural ingredients from Earth's soil, such as coal or copper, that come from the ground and are not plants, animals, or other living things.

population (pop-yoo-LAY-shun) The number of people who live in a region.

rain forests (RAYN FOR-ests) Very wet areas that have many kinds of plants, trees, and animals.

tropics (TRAH-piks) The warm parts of Earth that are near the equator.

File   Edit   View   Go   Bookmarks   Communicator   Help   2:37 PM

Back   Forward   Reload   Home   Search   Images   Print   Security   Stop

Netsite: What's Related

Index

A
agriculture, 18
Amazon River, 5
Andes mountain range,
    5, 9, 13
Atacama Desert, 9

C
Carnival, 5, 21
climate, 9, 13

E
equator, 9

H
hyperlinks, 5

I
industries, 18
Isthmus of Panama, 6

L
language, 17

M
mining, 18, 22

P
population, 10

R
rain forests, 9, 13, 14
religion, 17

S
search engine, 5

T
tango, the, 21
tropics, 9

Web Sites

Check out the exciting Web sites about South America on these
pages: pp, 7, 8, 11, 12, 15, 16, 19, 20, and 22.

24